INVOICE PRINTABLES

OVER 20 TO CHOOSE FROM

Excellent for

Contractors
Retailers
Wholesalers
Home Service
Professional Services

INVOICE

Company	INVOICE
Address	
Address	

Phone

SOLD TO:

INVOICE #:
INVOICE DATE:
ORDER #:

SHIPPED TO: Name

SALES REP:
SHIPPED VIA:
F.O.B:

Address City, State, Zip

Sales Tax Rate:

Quantity	Description	Unit Price	Amount
		Sub.Total	
		Tax	
		Freight	
		PAY THIS AMOUNT	

_____
_____
_____
_____

INVOICE

Date _____   **Invoice No.** _____

Customer   **Site**
Name _____   Address _____
Address _____   _____
_____   _____
Phone _____

Description	Amount
Subtotal	
Tax	
Shipping	
Total	

INVOICE

INVOICE NO. _____

DATE _____

_____
_____
_____
_____

SOLD TO

_____
_____
_____
_____

	QTY	UNIT	ITEM	PRICE	TOTAL
MATERIALS					
	QTY	UNIT	ITEM	PRICE	TOTAL
LABOR					

MATERIALS	
LABOR	
TAX	
TOTAL	

INVOICE

Date	Number

_____
_____
_____
_____

Sold To _____   Ship To _____
        _____   _____
        _____   _____
        _____   _____

Sold By	P.O Number	Date Shipped	Shipped Via	FOB Point	Terms

Job No.	Description	Rate	Hours	Total

	Subtotal	
	Tax	
	Shipping	
	Total	

INVOICE

INVOICE NO. _____

DATE _____

SOLD TO

	QTY	UNIT	ITEM	PRICE	TOTAL
MATERIALS					
	QTY	UNIT	ITEM	PRICE	TOTAL
LABOR					

MATERIALS	
LABOR	
TAX	
TOTAL	

INVOICE

INVOICE NO. _____

DATE _____

SOLD TO

QTY	UNIT	ITEM	PRICE	TOTAL

SUBTOTAL	
OTHER	
TAX	
TOTAL	

INVOICE

INVOICE NO. _____

DATE _____

ACCOUNT NAME

DESCRIPTION	CODE	PROVIDER	CHARGE

CHARGES _____

ADJUSTMENTS _____

TOTAL _____

Progress Payment Invoice

Company Name: _____
Address: _____
Address: _____
Phone: _____

Customer		Invoice No.
_____		Date
_____		
_____		Order No.
_____		

Last Payment Amount: _____ Date Paid: _____

Total Amt. Paid: _____

INVOICE

SKU	Description	Price	QTY	Total

Subtotal	
Tax	
Amt. Paid	
Total Due	

INVOICE

INVOICE NO. _____

DATE _____

SOLD TO

QTY	UNIT	ITEM	PRICE	TOTAL

SUBTOTAL	
OTHER	
TAX	
TOTAL	

INVOICE

TRASH REMOVAL

SOLD TO

INVOICE NO. _____

DATE _____

QTY	UNIT	ITEM	PRICE	TOTAL

SUBTOTAL

OTHER

TAX

TOTAL

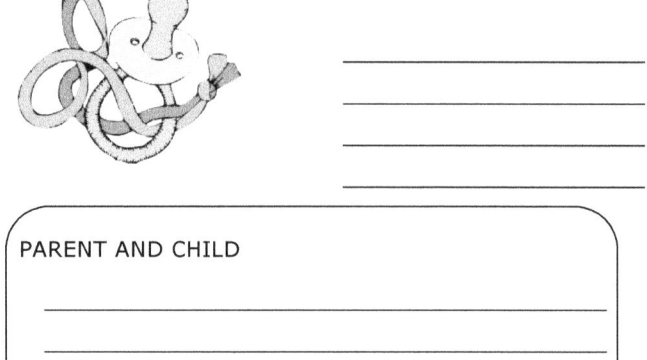

INVOICE

INVOICE NO. _____

DATE _____

PARENT AND CHILD

_____
_____
_____
_____

DAY	DESCRIPTION	RATE	HOURS	MEALS, GAS, ETC.	TOTAL

TOTAL [   ]

	INVOICE	
	Date	Number

Sold To _____

_____

_____

_____

Ship To _____

_____

_____

_____

Sold By	P.O Number	Date Shipped	Shipped Via	FOB Point	Terms

SKU	Description	Unit Price	Quantity	Total
			Subtotal	
			Tax	
			Shipping	
			Total	

INVOICE

Invoice No	
Date	

Sold To

Description	Hours	Rate	Total
		Total	

STATEMENT

Date _____

_____

_____

_____

_____

Bill To

_____

_____

_____

_____

Ship To

_____

_____

_____

_____

Date	Invoice / Description	Charge	Credit	Total
			Total	

_____
_____
_____
_____
_____

Sold To

_____   Invoice No   _____
_____   Date   _____
_____   Terms   _____
_____

Date	Description	Amount
	Total	

INVOICE

Invoice No.			Ship Via	
Date			Terms	

Bill To

_____

_____

_____

Ship To

_____

_____

_____

Number	Description	Unit Price	Amount
		Total	

ESTIMATE

COMPANY

_____

CLIENT

ADDRESS

_____

_____

_____

_____

_____

_____

JOB DESCRIPTION

ESTIMATED JOB COST _____

SUBMITTED BY

Sold To

Invoice No
Date
Terms

Date	Description	Amount
	Total	

INVOICE

SOLD TO

INVOICE NO. _____

DATE _____

	QTY	UNIT	ITEM	PRICE	TOTAL
MATERIALS					
	QTY	UNIT	ITEM	PRICE	TOTAL
LABOR					

MATERIALS	
LABOR	
TAX	
TOTAL	

PROPOSAL

COMPANY

_____

_____

CLIENT

_____

_____

TODAY'S DATE   JOB NAME

We propose to furnish the material and labor necessary to complete:

For the sum of: _____ $ _____

Payable as follows: _____

_____

Authorized Signature   _____ Date _____

Accepted _____ Date _____

Accepted _____ Date _____

WORK BID

COMPANY
_____
_____

CLIENT
_____
_____

We propose to supply all materials and labor necessary to complete the following:

NUMBER	DESCRIPTION	AMOUNT

INVOICE

INVOICE NO. _____

DATE _____

SOLD TO

QTY	UNIT	ITEM	PRICE	TOTAL

SUBTOTAL	
OTHER	
TAX	
TOTAL	

INVENTORY

COMPANY
NAME _____
ADDRESS _____

DATE _____
COUNTED BY _____

ITEM	NUMBER	UNIT	PRICE	TOTAL	NOTES

INVOICE

INVOICE NO. _____

DATE _____

SOLD TO

QTY	UNIT	ITEM	PRICE	TOTAL

SUBTOTAL	
OTHER	
TAX	
TOTAL	

www.ingramcontent.com/pod-product-compliance
Lightning Source LLC
Chambersburg PA
CBHW081822170526
45167CB00008B/3513